Fifty Years of Historic Lodging
and Waterfront Dining

By
Stafford and Janice Smith
and
Stafford's Hospitality, Inc.

Stafford's Hospitality

Fifty Years of Historic Lodging and Waterfront Dining

Dedication

To our guests, employees, communities, and friends who have made the last fifty years memorable and successful. Here's to fifty more!

The Donning Company Publishers
184 Business Park Drive, Suite 206
Virginia Beach, VA 23462

Steve Mull, General Manager

Barbara Buchanan, Office Manager

Anne Burns, Editor

Nathan Stufflebean, Graphic Designer

Priscilla Odango, Imaging Artist

Steve Hartman, Project Research Coordinator

Tonya Washam, Marketing Specialist

Pamela Engelhard, Marketing Advisor

G. Bradley Martin, Project Director

Library of Congress Cataloging-in-Publication Data

Smith, Stafford, 1938-

  Stafford's Hospitality : fifty years of historic lodging and waterfront dining / by Stafford and Janice Smith and Stafford's Hospitality, Inc.

     p. cm.

  ISBN 978-1-57864-674-6

1. Stafford's Hospitality, Inc.--History. 2. Historic hotels--Michigan--Petoskey--History. 3. Restaurants--Michigan--Petoskey--History. 4. Smith, Stafford, 1938- 5. Smith, Janice, 1939- I. Smith, Stafford, 1938- II. Stafford's Hospitality, Inc. III. Title.

  TX941.S73S65 2011

  647.95774'88--dc22

                              2011002637

Printed in the United States of America at Walsworth Publishing Company

Table of Contents

Stafford and Janice's Story

Fifty years! Goodness, how did that happen? It was only yesterday when we met!

Stafford and I stand in amazement as we look back over the last fifty years of becoming Stafford's Hospitality. Our bodies have changed, but our minds have not. Would we do it all over again? Wholeheartedly!

Many know our story. We met at the Bay View Inn during the summer of 1960. Stafford was the assistant manager and had worked for Dr. Roy Heath since the summer of 1957. I was the newly hired dining room hostess, sight unseen but highly recommended by the chef, Lois Clippard, who had known me since my birth. My first sight of Stafford, "Duff," was at my entrance into the inn. He was coming down the lobby stairs with a toilet seat over his head and one dangling from each arm. Not a charming way to meet your future husband.

He, however, had already seen me via my application photo, which he had placed in his wallet where it still resides. Dr. Heath had sent my application to Duff, who was in his senior year at Northwestern University, to inform him of my coming. Dr. Heath had asked Stafford to return to the inn as the assistant manager for one last summer before he started his career in labor arbitration, his field of study. Dr. Heath himself was making a career change and needed someone to run the hotel during his frequent absences.

As the summer unfolded, Stafford and I fell in love, not only with each other, but also with the area. We were destined to be in Petoskey, but we did

Stafford and
Janice Smith,
1963.

not understand that destiny until December 1960. In September, I returned for my senior year at Florence State College, now the University of North Alabama. Duff joined the ranks of recent college graduates looking for work. The year 1960 offered little opportunity for labor arbitrators, so he became an apprentice to Mr. John Daniels of Albion, Michigan, Stafford's hometown, who taught him to paint and wallpaper. Those skills were put to use quite often during constant years of refurbishing the inn. In fact, the wallpaper currently in the lobby of the Bay View Inn was one of his last applications. I can safely state that Duff has wallpapered the entire inn at least twice between the spring of 1961 and today. But, I am a little ahead of the story.

In December of 1960, Stafford was employed by Herbert Reycraft to become manager of the Perry Hotel. Herbert was the nephew of the Drs. Reycraft who purchased the hotel in 1917 and had hired their nephew to manage it for them. Upon their death, Herbert inherited the hotel. Duff had to convince Mr. Reycraft to hire him and that he had the knowledge and experience to operate his hotel. However, in April of 1961, Mr. Reycraft sold the Perry to John R. Davis, and Duff's position was terminated. I, however, had already been hired to teach in the Littlefield Public Schools in Alanson.

This is the time when "fate" stepped in. Duff was living with his brother Paul and his wife Nancy in Petoskey. They all knew Dr. Heath was trying to sell the Bay View Inn but had not been successful. Paul convinced Duff to call Dr. Heath and offer to run the inn for the summer until a buyer could be found. Dr. Heath had other plans. He told Duff to come to see him, and when Duff returned to Petoskey a few days later, he had a land contract of two pages to purchase the Bay View Inn. Now, he too, had a job, so my mother no longer had to worry about how Stafford was going to support a wife.

Here we were! Two twenty-two-year-old *youngsters,* by some standards, ready to embark on a career in hospitality. Just exactly what had we gotten ourselves into?

We've added other properties to our holdings in the course of fifty years. Currently we own and operate the Pier Restaurant which came on board in 1970, the Weathervane Restaurant was purchased in 1988, and the Perry Hotel became ours in 1989. We invite you to read on as we share our story.

Stafford and Janice Smith

The Smith Family (2011). Left to right: front, Andrew, Jessica, Kaitlyn, and Dean; middle, Lori, Stafford, Janice, and Mary-Kathryn; back, Reginald and Todd.

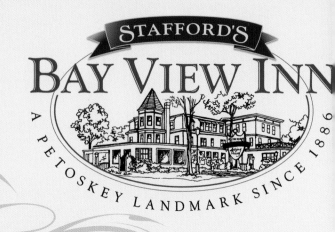

A Brief History of the Bay View Inn

In 1886, John Wesly Howard built the Woodland Avenue House in the fast-growing Methodist summer community of Bay View. The vibrant summer hotel was then renamed the Howard House in 1888. At that time, weekly rates averaged $4.50 for room and board. The property expanded throughout the years and assumed a number of different owners and names including the Roselawn. The inn was renamed once again in 1935 with the title it proudly displays today, the Bay View Inn.

Bay View Inn, 1918.

Original Bay View Inn, then called "the Howard House," circa 1886.

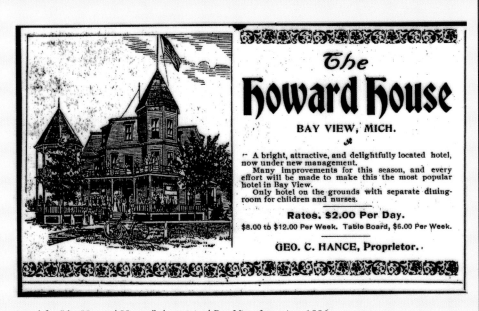

The Howard House

BAY VIEW, MICH.

A bright, attractive, and delightfully located hotel, now under new management.

Many improvements for this season, and every effort will be made to make this the most popular hotel in Bay View.

Only hotel on the grounds with separate dining-room for children and nurses.

Rates. $2.00 Per Day.

$8.00 to $12.00 Per Week. Table Board, $6.00 Per Week.

GEO. C. HANCE, Proprietor.

An ad for "the Howard House," the original Bay View Inn, circa 1886.

1961: The Beginning of Stafford's Hospitality

Above:
Stafford and
Janice Smith,
circa 1961.

Below:
Stafford and
Janice Smith,
2011.

What Stafford and Janice purchased was a summer hotel with sixty sleeping rooms—a big cottage really—no foundation walls except under the wing addition and the kitchen. The lobby and the front porch were supported by cedar posts. No insulation, no central heating, nor air-conditioning existed. The warmth or coolness inside the inn was strictly dependent on Mother Nature.

Electricity on the first and second floor rooms was modern for the time, but the third floor rooms were lit by a single light bulb dangling from a double strand, knob, and spool system of wiring. Most rooms were without baths but did have washbasins. Guests were afforded full baths down the hall. The inn was originally built as a boarding house with a large dining room and kitchen. For the Smiths, that dining room was a godsend as they soon learned it would increase their prosperity through food sales.

Stafford's clientele consisted of retired schoolteachers, widows, and ministers' wives who stayed the entire summer season. They would arrive by train in mid-June and return south when the programs in Bay View ended. The inn closed on Labor Day—Janice started teaching and Duff was out of a job once again each fall.

12

It became quite obvious this way of life was not going to be economically successful for very long. The passenger trains stopped running, vacationers were not staying in one place for more than three nights, and everyone wanted a private bath. Stafford and Janice had to change the inn's business model. Perhaps that factor is the major reason for the continued success. Stafford's Hospitality continues to change to meet the demands of its clientele.

As had previous owners, Stafford began putting his own stamp of proprietorship on the inn his very first summer. He went to task refurbishing the lobby. Working with his brother Paul, an interior decorator, Stafford tore out the old front desk, installed wainscoting, replaced the draperies, and hung new wallpaper. As the guests returned in the summer of 1961, they definitely knew new leadership was on board.

In 1962, guests discovered a freshly decorated dining room. No longer were they surrounded by dark wallpaper and a green linoleum floor. They were welcomed by bright, new bayside windows, white wainscoting, and gold, fuzzy eagles on the wallpaper.

Stafford Smith, circa 1970.

Stafford's first rebuilding project was to replace the sun parlor, which had been added to the hotel in 1923. His uncle Frank E. Dean, an architect in Albion, Michigan, redesigned the entire street side of the hotel, adding seventeen feet to the dining room. In addition to the new bay window, the dining room was now

Bay View Inn lobby—Stafford's first renovation, circa 1962.

14

carpeted. Also, during that early spring in 1963, guest rooms were renovated. Each spring, several rooms were singled out for new wallpaper and paint. Many of the smaller rooms were combined in order to add private baths, which provided the plumbers and electricians with quite a challenge.

By the late 60s, it became apparent to Stafford that minor cosmetic surgery to the inn would no longer suffice. If his dream to expand the hotel business to capture part of the growing winter market was to continue, major reconstruction of the hotel itself was necessary. Central heating, and eventually central air-conditioning, needed to be installed. Those amenities required insulation blown in from the third floor. This additional weight, and the fact the inn is on top of a shale ridge built up during the ice age and the retreating of Lake Michigan, resulted in sagging, creating cracks in the ceiling and walls of the inn. To

Stafford Smith carving at Sunday Brunch.

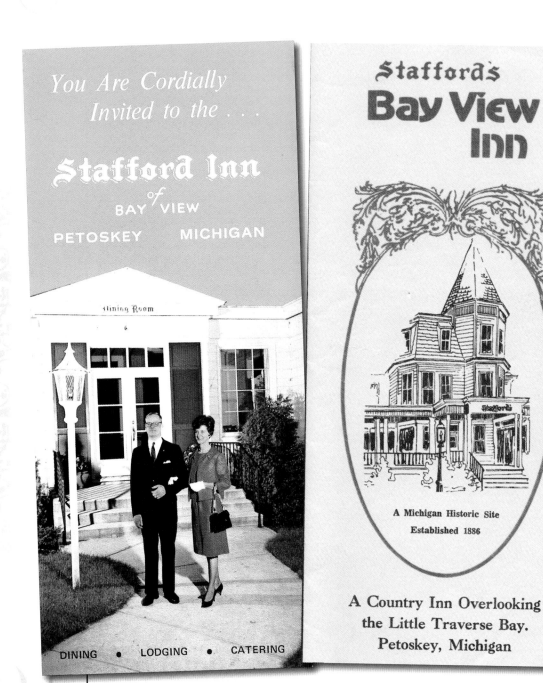

You Are Cordially
Invited to the . . .

Stafford Inn
of
BAY VIEW

PETOSKEY   MICHIGAN

DINING • LODGING • CATERING

Stafford's
Bay View
Inn

A Michigan Historic Site
Established 1886

A Country Inn Overlooking
the Little Traverse Bay.
Petoskey, Michigan

Early Bay View Inn brochures.

alleviate this problem, the third floor was abandoned and eventually gutted. All lath and plaster were removed. All pipes were capped. What remained was a super large storage space.

After a vote of the membership of the Bay View Association in the summer of 1968, the inn was allowed to stay open for winter occupancy. Stafford tested that market during the winter of 1968 only opening for the Christmas to New Year holiday. Beginning with the winter of 1969, the inn remained open on weekends only for the winter ski season.

Stafford's Bay View Inn might have remained just an interesting, quaint, summer hotel if Stafford had not met Norman Simpson, author of *Country Inns and Backroads* and founder of the country inn movement in the late 60s. Mr. Simpson stopped by the inn in 1970 at the recommendation of Stafford's brother Dean.

Mr. Simpson had admired the work Stafford and Janice were doing. During his visit, he offered many suggestions regarding the kind of service and trends that guests expected during a stay in a country inn. Warm hospitality, good food—preferably served on the premises—and cozy but well-lit public areas where guests could congregate to talk or read were a few of his recommendations for an award-winning inn. In addition, he pointed out that travelers seeking unique accommodations, not cookie cutter rooms with synthetic plants in the corner, were turning to inns for comfort and old-fashion service and friendship. Stafford became part of Norman Simpson's innkeeping family in 1972 and has remained a member ever since.

To be included in Mr. Simpson's guidebook of inns, the Bay View Inn had to meet certain qualifications. In addition to the general standards of cleanliness and friendly hospitality, each inn must provide breakfast and dinner either on the premises or in walking distance. Mr. Simpson did not want guests to have to drive to obtain refreshment. Lobbies large enough for guests to meet each

Bay View Inn staff, circa 1985.

other in discourse, reading lamps next to chairs or bedside, and innkeepers present on property were also provisions for membership. Inns and innkeepers were to provide guests an experience in warmth and hospitality not just a room with a bed.

The Bay View Inn became a member of this guidebook in 1972. This organization has evolved into the renowned SELECT REGISTRY, Distinguished Inns of North America, which boasts a membership of over four hundred of the finest country inns, luxury bed and breakfasts, and unique small hotels in North America. The quality assurance program for membership is based on Norman Simpson's original qualifications. Stafford was picked by Norman to be the first president of this new association in 1984, a position he continued to hold in 1985 and 1986.

In 1977, Stafford began to reconstruct the inn's foundation. By that time, Louie Bandemer joined the staff as resident builder. Louie, along with John Still, hand dug the central part of the building. The front porch was removed, a foundation was poured, and the porch was rebuilt. Part of this porch became the expanded Roselawn Porch dining room. The room was reconfigured in the mid-80s when "Rooms A and B" were incorporated into the dining area. The other dining rooms and lobby were also remodeled and the hotel's décor returned to its cottage Victorian heritage. The colonial eagle motif returned to the eastern colonies where it belonged.

The third floor was rebuilt in the 1980s and 1990s. The renovation of the original structure in the front of the inn was completed in 1986, in time for Janice and Stafford's twenty-fifth wedding anniversary.

The Bay View Inn now has thirty-one guest rooms with private baths, some with Jacuzzis, fireplaces, and parlors. For safety purposes, the entire inn is protected by a sprinkler system. It is a premier Victorian inn and the longest continuously operated summer hotel, now year round, north of Grand Rapids. It is a Michigan Historic Site within the National Historic District of Bay View, Michigan.

Above: Bay View Inn employees Judy H., Keri V., and Kathy H., circa 1982.

Left: Bay View Inn, 2011.

Bay View Inn
lobby.

STAFFORD'S
BAY VIEW INN

J. W. Howard completed this spacious inn in 1887, naming it the Woodland Avenue House because of its proximity to that street. Later he called the hotel the Howard House. In 1923 the popular resort became the Roselawn in honor of Horace Rose, innkeeper at that time. Renamed the Bay View Inn, this building is now Stafford's Bay View Inn and is one of the oldest seasonal hotels in continuous operation in the area. Carved out of deeded railroad property next to the village of Petoskey in 1875, the summer colony of Bay View began as a religious retreat. Then it became a cultural and educational center complete with a college and Chautauqua series. This inn is a center of hospitality in the swirl of local summer activities.

The Bay View Inn is a Michigan Historic Site within the National Historic District of Bay View, Michigan.

Catering

As mentioned before, Stafford's business model had to change in order to maintain a viable operation. Stafford's started a catering unit in 1968, by serving a number of mid-morning "coffees" for the ladies of Bay View. It was popular for the women to invite their friends over for coffee following the morning lecture at Voorhies Hall, so Stafford and Janice created the menus and transported the "goodies" to the cottages. Janice would load up her station wagon, arrange the sweets and tea sandwiches, and serve the coffee.

Word spread and soon Stafford's was traveling to Walloon Lake to serve brunches. Many "black-outs" occurred in these cottages due to Stafford's plugged-in griddles and coffee pots. These small opportunities developed into Stafford's becoming the caterers of the Walloon Lake Country Club for a number of years.

The first catering job of an entire meal, including food, dishes, silver, etc., came from a conversation with Warren Luttmann, superintendent of Petoskey Public Schools in 1968.

"Stafford, could you cater the opening of the new Petoskey High School with a meeting of the Rotary Club in our cafeteria?" asked Warren.
"Sure," replied Stafford.

Stafford and Janice borrowed brother Paul's van, loaded up the food and dishes, and headed up the hill. They did not think about tying anything down. They had the food in the cart, but had placed the butter plates, already filled with butter, on a tray on top of the cart. Well, as they started up the hill, the butter started down. This mishap is only one among many that were part of Stafford and Janice's learning their business with "on the job" training.

The second venture then, in the future establishment of Stafford's Hospitality, was catering. Stafford and Janice did a lot of catering and still do some. Tents were purchased and special equipment and trucks were bought solely for that purpose. Whenever anyone called about bringing a meal or doing a party for them, Stafford and Janice said they would be happy to. They even traveled to cities downstate.

Two famous caters have to be mentioned. President Ford was to visit Mackinac Island one summer during his presidency. Stafford's was asked to cater *Air Force One* for its return trip to Washington, D.C. They went to Pellston, loaded up the special dishware provided by the crew, cooked the meal (medallions of beef tenderloin), packed it up, and took it to the plane. No security check!!

The other catering operation did not go so smoothly. The new cement plant in Charlevoix was to open and the officials wanted to have a big gala for the dedication. Governor Romney was to be the speaker and dignitaries from all the local governments were to be invited. The officials called and asked if Stafford's would pit roast a buffalo. Once again, Stafford said "Sure!" He hung up the phone and asked Janice to research how to roast a buffalo.

As it turned out, roasting a buffalo was not so simple. The occasion became a hot dog, potato salad, and baked beans picnic for the public. All hands were on deck again as plans were made to serve two thousand. Even some houseguests peeled potatoes in the back room. New food carriers were bought for the potato salad and baked beans, but just as soon as the hot baked beans were poured into the container, which was plastic, it melted and the beans spilled all over the floor! An order had been placed for 144 dozen hot dog buns from the bread man, but he only delivered 12 dozen, thinking the order was a mistake. When the company was called in a panic, the salesman raided every grocery store from Petoskey to Mackinaw City to secure enough buns.

To make matters worse, Stafford's also ordered charcoal from a local coal company. When the charcoal was lit, a dark black cloud filled the sky. The company had delivered coal. If anyone in Charlevoix wanted to purchase charcoal that weekend, they would not find it, as Stafford's purchased every bag available. All went well after that, but the Smith family and their neighbors ate hot dogs at least once a week all winter.

Stafford Smith and Dudley Marvin Partnership

No business is successful without outstanding employees. The most extraordinary employee story is the one concerning the hiring of Dudley Marvin. Stafford's Hospitality has had many long-term employees; however, Dudley is the most important of all.

Before the Bay View Inn became a year-round operation, Stafford was hired by Boyne USA Resorts to open its dining room at the new Boyne Highlands operation. This position required him to hire all winter personnel for the dining room. He visited several campuses to interview students for these positions.

On the day President Kennedy was shot, Stafford interviewed Dudley Marvin at Wayne State University to become a busboy. During Dudley's tenure at Boyne, Stafford convinced him to transfer to Michigan State University (MSU) and to change his major to hospitality during college. Dudley continued to work at the Bay View Inn, doing everything from cleaning the rooms to cooking breakfast. He met two of his lifelong friends while working there the first summer, Oatfield

Dudley Marvin and Stafford Smith, circa 1985.

W. Whitney III and John C. Smith. Dudley continued to work at the inn for three straight summers during college, and he always liked the Smith family. One summer, Stafford's mother told Dudley she liked the work he was doing and gave him $100 towards his books for the upcoming semester.

During the winter of 1966, Stafford had a contract with Earl Young in Charlevoix to run his dining room. Stafford called Dudley and asked him to bring staff from MSU to help. Dudley gathered up friends and roommates for bartenders, waitstaff, etc. and they headed to Charlevoix to work.

"I remember meeting Earl Young," Dudley said. "He said to me 'You want to be in the restaurant business? It's a business of details.'" Earl continued to speak and grabbed Dudley by the ear, "The signs and lights HAVE to be on. If they are not on, turn them on. Son, it's a business of details."

Dudley and Darlene Marvin with Janice and Stafford Smith at one of the company's first annual guest appreciation parties, circa 1988.

Shortly after he finished college, Dudley went on to the navy where he was commissioned as an ensign in the United States Naval Reserve. Just before he was out of the navy, he met his wife, Darlene D'Anzi, out in California.

In February of 1970, Stafford had just purchased a share of the Pier Restaurant in Harbor Springs. Dudley knew he wanted to come back to northern Michigan so he called Stafford. Stafford told Dudley, "If you come here to run it, I will buy it." Dudley began managing the Pier Restaurant in the spring of 1970.

Dudley was instrumental at Stafford's Pier. He established a culture of service, reminding his staff daily, "We never let an unhappy customer leave. If the customer gives you a hard time, just be nicer!" His staff stood behind him and became number one in customer service in northern Michigan.

Dudley became president of Stafford's Hospitality in 1981 and still remains its president today.

The Marvin Family. Front row: Brady and Allie. Middle row: Dudley holding Konner, Darlene holding Noah, Dudley (Joey), Reese, and Devin. Back row: Debi (Marvin), Dan, Jodie, Dudley III, David, and Audrey. Not pictured: Kendal Shirley (born January 4, 2011).

STAFFORD'S PIER RESTAURANT

A HARBOR SPRINGS LANDMARK SINCE 1935

Stafford's Pier Restaurant

Up until March 1970, Stafford's Hospitality consisted of two entities: Stafford's Bay View Inn and Stafford's Catering. Even though the inn was now open on winter weekends for ski season, it really wasn't a year round operation.

One important lesson Stafford and Janice learned during their "on the job training" is that the salesman who services the hospitality industry knows what the *scuttlebutt* is in any restaurant in the area. Pete Campbell, a purveyor for Pfelzer Brothers, a Chicago Stock Yard company, informed Stafford that one of the partners was interested in selling his share of the Pier Restaurant. Stafford did not want all of his eggs in one basket. He purchased Basil Thompson's interest in the Pier and became the operating partner with Ward Walstrom. Ten years later, Stafford became the sole owner.

The Pier is also an historic property as are all of Stafford's establishments. Built before prohibition, the original structure consisted only of the current Chart Room which was named the Pier Bar and Grill.

Ward Walstrom and Basil Thompson purchased the restaurant in 1967 and redesigned the Chart Room structure, which became the Stein Room so named after Basil's collection of beer steins. The two new owners proceeded

The Pier, circa 1980.

Pier Bar, circa
1945.

Harbor
Springs, circa
1945.

Stafford's
Pointer Room,
circa 1982.

The Pointer,
circa 1980s.

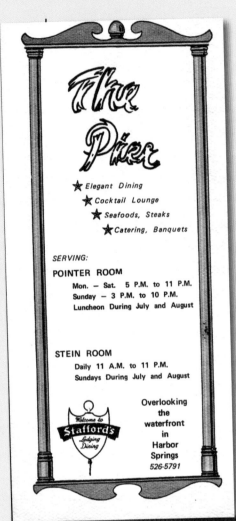

The Pier

★ *Elegant Dining*
★ *Cocktail Lounge*
★ *Seafoods, Steaks*
★ *Catering, Banquets*

SERVING:

POINTER ROOM
Mon. — Sat. 5 P.M. to 11 P.M.
Sunday — 3 P.M. to 10 P.M.
Luncheon During July and August

STEIN ROOM
Daily 11 A.M. to 11 P.M.
Sundays During July and August

Welcome to
Stafford's
Lodging Dining

Overlooking
the
waterfront
in
Harbor
Springs
526-5791

DANCING

EVERY
WEDNESDAY, SATURDAY
AND SUNDAY NIGHTS

AL'S *at the Pier*

Harbor Springs

Above: Pier Restaurant ad, circa 1970.

Right: Early Pier Restaurant ad, circa 1945.

to design an upscale dining room, the Pointer Room, which occupied the space over the boathouse for *The Pointer*, a taxi boat that previously served the Harbor Point community.

A very devastating situation occurred that summer. The Pointer Room was scheduled to open in May of 1968, but an area-wide strike by the bricklayer's union delayed the opening until mid-August. This strike affected the whole area from Traverse City to Cheboygan. The staff had already been hired and had to be paid even though the dining room was not open for business. A whole season was lost due to this strike.

The Pointer Room is built over the water and required the service of the Army Corps of Engineers. Seventy-five-feet pilings were planted in the waters of the harbor in preparation for the room's foundation. This dining room affords a panoramic view of the harbor. Stafford and Ward added the Wheelhouse Lounge in the early 70s to combine the Pointer Room bar and Chart Room bar into one entity in order to provide more dining space.

Gazing out the window of the Pointer Room, customers can see *The Pointer*.

Stafford and Dudley were shamed into purchasing this boat. The "Coffee Club," a group of local businessmen who met in the Chart Room every morning for coffee, pushed for the purchase. They knew *The Pointer* was stored in a barn north of Harbor Springs. It was in poor condition, and the purchase price did not include restoration. VanDam Boat Works restored the boat in 1989 and it has been in the water since.

Today, Stafford's Pier consists of four dining rooms—the Wheelhouse Lounge, the Chart Room, the Pointer Room, and Dudley's Deck.

Dudley's Deck at Stafford's Pier Restaurant.

Stafford's Pier Restaurant and *The Pointer*, 2011.

Stafford's Weathervane Restaurant— Much More Than a Mill

When Dudley came on board, Stafford turned over the operation of the Pier Restaurant to him. One of Stafford's principles in business is if he hires a person to manage a property, he lets that manager operate the property as if it were his own. If guidance is needed, he will provide guidance. If a situation evolves that requires a change in managers, then he will separate from that manager on good terms. In Dudley's case, he is still very much involved in Stafford's Hospitality.

Stafford once operated the Weathervane for the owner, Earl Young, during the winter of 1965–66. It was a disastrous winter as little snow fell. In fact, people played golf and water-skied on Little Traverse Bay on January 1, 1966.

That spring, Stafford's tried to purchase the restaurant but an agreement could not be reached at that time. The restaurant was later sold to other operators, none of whom were able to make a success of the business, as it is very difficult to operate any restaurant or hotel in a highly seasonal resort culture.

The situation changed in the spring of 1988. Stafford was attending a meeting of independent innkeepers in Minnesota when Dudley called him.

Pine River,
Charlevoix,
date unknown.

"Stafford, Mr. Jon Hisey, Bill Martin's partner, is in my office, and Mr. Hisey says that he will not leave my office until I agree to take over the operation of the Weathervane restaurant. He is not asking us to purchase the property, but wants our corporation to lease the business. What would you like me to do?" Dudley asked.

"Well, Dudley, what do you think?" Stafford asked.

"It might be a good opportunity," Dudley said.

"Okay, go ahead. Have a lease drawn up, and if it is reasonable, we will do it. How soon does he want us to take over?" Stafford said.

"Tomorrow!" Dudley replied.

The Weathervane was added to Stafford's Hospitality in May of 1988. It, too, is an historic property on the water. Originally the building was a gristmill where farmers could sell their grain. Schooners which plied the Great Lakes could easily load the flour to transport to the many harbors on the lakes.

Right: The Weathervane, circa 1989.

Below: Weathervane's fireplace.

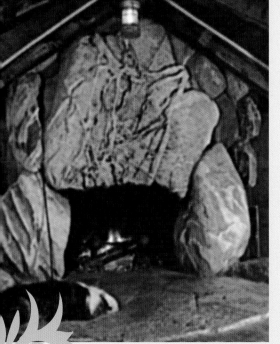

During the post-war years, when men and materials were once more available for civilian projects, Charlevoix realtor Earl Young acquired the mill and transformed it into a restaurant, which opened in 1954. The top two floors were eliminated, and the new roof was fashioned after the curve of a gull's wing. The building was faced with limestone and trimmed with Onaway stone from the local quarry. Young filled the restaurant with nautical memorabilia, some of which can still be seen throughout.

Characteristic of Young's imaginative stonework is the glacial boulder located in the main dining room. Found by Young in the

38

Charlevoix area, the nine-ton keystone in the fireplace resembles the mitten of Michigan's Lower Peninsula. The meteorite lying at the hearth is only a quarter of the size of the keystone, but it weighs the same.

Jeff's Deck at Stafford's Weathervane, 2011.

The main bar is constructed of shipwrecked planks weighing over two tons. Illuminating the Weathervane's entrance are two 150-year-old streetlights imported from Copenhagen. The circular stairwell to the lower level is another testimony to Young's creativity. This intimate lower room is comprised of massive timbers as beams and another stone fireplace. The outside wall opens to the outdoors where diners can watch the boats sail through the channel into Round Lake.

Stafford's mark on this historic landmark is the deck of outside dining added in 2006. This addition is the same as if adding a whole new dining room, doubling the dining capacity during the summer months.

Stafford's
Weathervane
Restaurant,
2011.

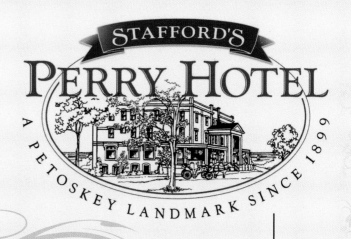

STAFFORD'S
PERRY HOTEL
A PETOSKEY LANDMARK SINCE 1899

Stafford's Perry Hotel— A Pioneer in Elegant Lodging

Even though Stafford's position at the Perry Hotel was eliminated in 1961, he had dreams of one day owning that hotel. He tried on several occasions to purchase the property, but again could not work out an acceptable arrangement. However in 1989, the Perry-Davis, its name since 1961, was in bankruptcy. The developer who had purchased the business in 1987 fell into financial ruin, and Old Kent Bank of Petoskey was in first position to receive the hotel. Following the court hearing, the officers of the bank approached Stafford to buy the hotel from them. At first, Stafford just wanted to lease the hotel under a similar contract designed for the Weathervane Restaurant. Banks do not lease properties returned to them by default, so a generous purchase agreement was drawn up and Stafford's Hospitality became the owner of the Perry. A dream had come true.

Norman J. Perry built this hotel and opened its doors in July of 1899. It was the first brick, fireproof hotel constructed in Petoskey, and the last of the pioneer hotels to be built in the region. Due to the number of fires in the city in the 1880s, city ordinances would no longer permit construction of wooden hotels. One fire in particular, the Farmer's Home on Lake Street, burned in 1880 and took down most of the block.

Perry Hotel
lobby, circa
1899.

Perry Hotel
bar, circa
1990.

Tourism began in Petoskey with the expansion of the Grand Rapids and Indiana Railroad in November of 1873. The first hotel of any consequence was built in 1874 and named the Rose House in honor of the entrepreneur Hiram Obed Rose, founder of the limestone industry here and Petoskey's first mayor. If Bear Creek, the name of the original settlement, had not been named after Ottawa Indian Chief Pe-to-se-ga, which was H. O. Rose's suggestion, it would have been named Rose Village. Four other major hotels (the Cushman, the Clifton, the Arlington, and the Imperial) were constructed within a block of each other between 1875 and 1895. The Imperial burned in 1898 and the Arlington, with its three hundred rooms, burned in 1915. Both the Clifton and the Cushman were torn down in the early 1900s as these buildings were no longer suitable for hotels. The Perry remains Petoskey's only downtown hotel.

Mr. Perry was not always in the hotel business. He was one of Petoskey's early dentists. A woman came into his office one day and asked to have

Hotel Perry, circa 1900.

43

Stafford's Perry Hotel, 2011.

eleven teeth pulled. A friend accompanied her to the office as she had a nervous, fidgety type personality. Dr. Perry administered some calming medication and pulled her teeth. She stood up, took a few steps, collapsed, and died. Following an investigation, Dr. Perry was absolved from any wrongdoing, but he decided to leave town and pursue a different career. Several years later, he returned to Petoskey and operated the Park House Hotel while his hotel was built across the street.

After World War I and subsequent economic downturns, the hotels in Petoskey were no longer viable businesses. The Clifton was sold in 1911 and torn down in 1917. The Cushman survived because of its reputation for food. Auto clubs would stop there to stay and dine and then move on. But it too, met the wrecking ball in the 1930s. Dr. Perry sold his hotel in 1919 to the Drs. John and George Reycraft who wished to turn it into a hospital. If that goal had been obtained, Petoskey would have been left without any downtown hotel.

The city businessmen pleaded with the doctors to maintain the building as a hotel. These city "fathers" believed, and justly so, that if Petoskey were to have a solid business community, it must have a substantial downtown hotel. The doctors agreed and purchased the Grand Hotel on Bear River for their hospital. They then hired their nephew Herbert Reycraft to operate the Perry Hotel. It was Herbert who hired Stafford to manage the Perry in 1961 and not long after, sold the hotel to John R. Davis, vice president of the Ford Motor Company.

Every time Stafford purchases a property, he puts his stamp on it from both a physical and service point of view. He strongly believes the physical plant of a

The Perry
Hotel's front
porch.

business reflects the owner's spirit and integrity. Before opening the Bay View
Inn in 1961, he completely remodeled the lobby. He did the same thing with
lobby of the Perry by having it painted Chinese red and fitted with new drapes.

The outside of the building was repainted only to find in two years the
paint was chipping off. This flecking was due to the spalling of the brick,
which was a poorly made, local brick. Several hundred bricks had to be
replaced and re-pointed. Following this procedure the hotel was painted with
a Sherwin-Williams paint developed for restoring old brick buildings such as
the Perry. The canary yellow paint was rolled on by hand.

The vision to add the Rose Garden Veranda came from Dudley and
Stafford while they were having lunch in the Rose Room one afternoon.
As they gazed out the window at the bay, a large delivery truck drove into
the parking lot and spoiled their view. They looked at each other and noted
that a change had to be made. Stafford traveled to England later that year,
and while there, discovered the conservatory. After considerable research
regarding snow loads, he ordered one from England. Maureen Parker

Right: Rose Garden Veranda, 2011.

Below: The Perry Hotel is a Michigan Historic Site within the National Historic District of downtown Petoskey.

and John Hoffman, local landscape architect and landscaper respectfully, designed the garden. This veranda is in constant demand for weddings.

Stafford feels honored to preserve and maintain the historic buildings that make up Stafford's Hospitality. He believes this preservation contributes to the viability of the community of which these buildings are a part. His restoration of the Bay View Inn influenced others to restore their cottages, and Stafford's Perry still stands as an anchor to the business community of Petoskey.

Stafford's Gallery of Art and History

Stafford's Gallery of Art and History was started in 2007. Formerly Longton Hall Antiques, Stafford's Gallery was a natural addition to Stafford's Perry Hotel (which is located adjacent to the gallery).

The gallery building was originally an icehouse in the 1930s. Ice from the Little Traverse Bay would be brought in and cut into large pieces and delivered to homes and shops for refrigeration. From there, it became Petoskey Packing Company where meat was packaged. Years later, it was an ice cream plant called Martin's Ice Cream. In 1969, the building became an antique shop,

Stafford's Hall
of History.

named Longton Hall, and remained so until 2007. Antiques were purchased from London, Scotland, and throughout the United States.

Stafford's Gallery offers a look back into Petoskey's olden days. Guests today can still walk through the freezer doors of the icehouse and look into different rooms that still have the original glazed block walls, ice chutes, and delivery entrances.

These characteristics make the perfect backdrop for displaying artwork as well as our Hall of History room, showcasing a collection of photos and artifacts representing the history of downtown Petoskey from the late 1800s to the early 1900s, with an emphasis on the twenty-two hotels that were once located downtown.

Stafford's Gallery showcases thirty-eight Michigan artists, featuring a variety of mediums including: watercolors, oils, photography, sculptures, jewelry, original and limited edition prints, gifts, accessories, and exquisite antiques.

Delightful Dining at Stafford's

No matter the era, no matter the proprietor, serving good food was always and remains a major portion of Stafford's Hospitality, and it all started at the Bay View Inn. Early advertisements for the inn made mention of "good, home cooking." When Stafford assumed the responsibility for the food program, he continued to emphasize this well-established tradition.

First Bay View Inn brunch, circa 1962.

One of the first traditions at the Bay View Inn was the Sunday Smorgasbord, started during Roy Heath's ownership and remains in place today as Stafford's famous Sunday Brunch, one of Michigan's best. The original, two-table buffet has been replaced by a wall-to-wall expansion of delectable entrées and side dishes.

The above photo was taken in 1962, just before the doors of the dining room were opened for the first buffet of the season. Featuring standing rib roast, turkey, and baked ham, guests would stroll down the table to help themselves to tomato pudding, sweet potatoes, fresh vegetables, and an array of homemade salads and relishes. Janice would greet over a hundred guests for each of the two Sunday buffets.

49

Above: Sunday Brunch, circa 1963.

Right: Stafford Smith.

Today, Stafford's Hospitality has ten dining rooms for their guests, with many of the very first recipes still being served including: Stafford's Classic Chicken Salad, Stafford's Seafood Chowder, Raspberry Vinaigrette Dressing, Oak Planked Whitefish, and Inn-made Sticky Buns. Many of the vegetables and seafood come from local vendors and farms, practicing the farm to table concept and promoting that Stafford's food is "always fresh, always fabulous."

50

Top: Oak Planked Whitefish.

Bottom: Stafford's Bibb Salad.

Guest Memories

In 2010, Stafford's held a memory contest asking guests to submit their favorite recollection of an overnight stay, dining experience, special event, or exemplary service at Stafford's. Here are a few of the favorites.

The Squirrel

Sometime on the morning of July 17, 2010, a squirrel crawled into a transformer and the power went down in the entire community of Bay View. I know this because that was the morning of my wedding, which was to take place later that day in the garden of Stafford's Bay View Inn, with 167 guests in attendance for the ceremony, cocktails and a scrumptious dinner showcasing Northern Michigan's finest local foods.

When I first awoke and looked at the clock that day, the glowing red dials said 5:30 a.m. I willed myself not to look again until a more reasonable hour, although I was so excited there was no way I was going back to sleep. When I did glance over again, there were no numbers at all. A little strange, but I didn't really dwell on it, focused instead on the fact that it was my wedding day!

I got up and skipped over and tried the light switch. Nothing. And then the water faucet. Still nothing. Hmmm. "Probably just something going on with our room, right?" I thought, as a little twinge of anxiety started to creep in. My trusty Maid-of-Honor, who was by my side, calmly suggested we go downstairs to see what was the matter. When what to our wondering eyes should appear, but darkened hallways everywhere and I really began to fear…

The lovely girl at the desk, who to her credit never lost her smile, Shared the news that made my heart beat fast for quite a while… A squirrel in the transformer, no power for miles, And no water to boot - how was I ever going to walk down that aisle? I'll stop rhyming now, as that's a different story, but just a peek at some of [the] thoughts racing through my mind would show you everything from "How would the chefs be able to cook?" to "How would we see?" to more immediately at the moment "How would I take a shower?"

Fortunately, I never had the opportunity to move into full-fledged panic mode, as help swooped in immediately, in the form of Mr. and Mrs. Stafford Smith. Right away, they reserved the spa at the Perry Hotel for my bridesmaids and me that morning. Mrs. Smith herself met us there and showed us around. As we got ready, she brought us coffee and muffins, along with the sweet, happy news that the transformer had been fixed and all was right in the wedding world again!

It went on to be the most beautiful July day, with calm skies and sun dancing on the water and in the garden - a perfect day for a wedding, as it turns out. And so the tale will be told for future years to come, of the squirrel who took down the transformer and Mr. and Mrs. Smith of Stafford's Bay View Inn, who saved the day. Just one more thing before I close – our Stafford's Bay View Inn story would not be complete without a last hurrah for Ms. Kristina Carlson, who made each and every day we worked with her the most perfect day to have a wedding. Our sincere thanks to all!

Kristin
Chicago, Illinois

Jim and Kristin on their wedding day.

The Big Shield

I was born in Muskegon in 1948, the fourth child of an eventual eight and our family, although not poor, lived with the cautious modesty of knowing that poor might be just a week or two away. Overnight vacations were few and frugal. When one did come along the station wagon would be filled with kids and excitement and the destination, always somewhere in Michigan, a Kernel of delight to be kept in mind as we traveled, counting the cows to left and right in competition and eagerly anticipating artesian wells and "Burma shave" signs. If we went north my father usually drove up US 131 which was then just a two-lane highway with plenty to see and places to pull over and take a look.

Each time we passed through Petoskey I would watch for two things in particular – the large area of exposed rock just north of the Perry hotel (which has since been covered) and what I called the "Big Shield", a little further up the road on the other side. It stood next to a large building with lots of windows and a little turret just above a porch.

My wife was also born in 1948 and during the sixteen years that passed before we met, I had gone by the "big shield", up and back probably a dozen times. We were married in 1970 and also took modest vacations, when we could. But that changed ten years later when my wife was looking through the February issue of Redbook Magazine and read to me several paragraphs from a glowing review of Sunday Brunch at Stafford's Bay View Inn, near Petoskey. The author was particularly partial to the tomato pudding. Not being spur-of-the-moment types, we decided to visit there come September, on Labor Day Weekend.

This was a step up for us – an "Inn"! Plus we intended to walk the Mackinac Bridge. As we drove through Petoskey that September, I once again admired the outcrop of stone while keeping an eye out for our Inn and, in a singular moment of interconnected memories as we neared the "big shield", I realized with childlike joy that that was where we were staying! As an extra serendipity our room was #1, just above the porch – the one with the little turret.

And yes, the brunch was fabulous, and has been many times since, although we only opted for the tomato pudding that first time!

James and Christine
Grand Haven, Michigan

Perry Hotel Memory

My most memorable stay was at the Perry Hotel in June of 2006. I was a member of John Demmer's group on hand to celebrate the reunion of John's World War II comrades. There were just three of John's original unit on hand, but also some widows and extended family members from various parts of the country. I recall that one of the small conference rooms on the lower level was reserved for their meeting & show memorabilia.

I was on hand as I play the bagpipes and piped the guests into the various venues during their stay. We all traveled by trolley buses and returned each night to the Perry Hotel.

That last evening, the final banquet was held on the Perry's large patio, where an excellent meal was served, and many "war stories" were told. In the enclosed photo taken there, we all wore "do-rags" made from table napkins in honor of the WWII mechanics headgear.

The service was excellent and the food exceptional, and I know that everyone had a wonderful time. I should mention that I am also employed at Demmer Corp. and John thought the pipes would lend a special touch to the occasion. He was right.

Terence
Okemos, Michigan

The Bay
View Inn
"Shield."

The Story Behind the Big Shield

The original Bay View Inn sign was developed by Stafford's brother Paul. Stafford wanted to establish a new identity for the Bay View Inn. He wanted to let the public know they were welcome. Many people had the mistaken notion that the Bay View community was private and the public was not welcome to its programs or buildings, which was not true then or now.

The sign also had to fit on or over the two posts that held a neon sign with Bay View Inn written on it. Stafford believed this signage was inappropriate for the Victorian inn. Paul created the shield, somewhat designed after a fraternity pin, featuring highly stylized lettering with two "backward Ns." It was built by Truman Cummings who was later contracted to rebuild the sunroom and dining room addition in 1963. The sign received a lot of interest and was featured in an article in the *Grand Rapids Press* in August of 1961 touting Stafford as the youngest innkeeper in Michigan.

Several years later, Ronald B. Hay, a graphic designer well known in automotive circles, stopped by the inn and inquired if he could redesign or embellish the shield with a new look. Ron was summering in the region and doing some work with a local photographer. He had worked for the Willy's Auto Company and then moved on to General Motors. He was famous for the current script logo *Cadillac* originating in the 1930s and still in use today. Ron was a very interesting man with whom Stafford's Hospitality developed a great friendship. He collected several antiques and gifted Stafford's with the stained glass windows that hang in the Roselawn Porch dining room.

Ron added the ribbon and new lettering on the shield. He, himself, cut out the letters, applied gold leaf, and placed them on the ribbon. That ribbon, with additional embellishments, has become the official logo of Stafford's Hospitality.

Exemplary Service

In the summer of 1972, I was hired by my neighbor, Dudley Marvin, to wait tables in the Chart Room of the Pier. This was before the days of the salad bar, and I think the Wheelhouse was not in operation yet. On Friday and Saturday Nights there were 3 waitresses scheduled to handle dinner in the Chart Room. It was a busy busy restaurant and we usually had people waiting to be seated. We usually did not have the help of a busboy unless Sally Case from the Pointer room could spare someone.

On this particular night, we were just packed. All of a sudden out of nowhere appeared a gentleman in a white bus coat, a little older than I was. He was pouring coffee, watering tables, clearing plates, busing tubs, he seemed to know just what to do without any direction. When I had a minute to finally thank him and compliment him, I said to him "Wow, you have been a tremendous help tonight. I would like to buy you a drink after work!" This gentleman responded with a big smile and said "No Penny, I will buy you a drink tonight....I am Stafford Smith".

I worked for Stafford and Jan for a couple of years. I worked in catering, Birchwood, and even at the Inn. As I learned from that night in the Chart room working for Stafford was totally a team effort. That team effort is the backbone of the "exemplary service" and Stafford's Hospitality.

Penny
Harbor Springs, Michigan

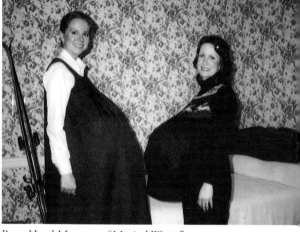

Perry Hotel Memory—"Magical Water."

Magical Water

My husband John and I, along with our dear friends, Tom and Lisa, will be celebrating our 27th year at the Perry Hotel, a cherished Super Bowl tradition since 1984.

As you can see by the 1984 photo Lisa (left) and I were also celebrating our first pregnancies in one of Perry Davis' beautiful Arlington rooms, exaggerated by stuffing a few pillows for added effect. What fun we had that first year, reading our baby books by the lobby's cozy fire as our husbands skied, vowing to return each Super Bowl Weekend, God willing. To our surprise, our girls, Jenny and Julie were born that June, delivered by the same doctor, only four days apart.

1989 was a special year as well. Not only did Stafford's purchase the Perry Hotel, but Lisa and I were gifted with the birth of our boys, Brian and Nick, delivered only five days apart. Rumor had it that there might have been something magical in that Perry water…

We look forward each year to sipping wine in the 3rd floor library, listening to Irish music in the Noggin Room Pub, those delicious breakfast sticky buns in the H.O. Rose Dining Room, and the fantastic service of the Perry staff, most particularly Mark, who never ages and keeps our water glasses filled to the brim.

Although Tom and Lisa have since moved to Greenwich, CT, our tradition still carries on. Thank you, Stafford's, for your gracious hospitality, for creating lasting memories, and for that magical water!

Nancy
Hastings, Michigan

The Stafford's Tradition Continues
by Janice Smith

Stafford and I have always worked side by side with our employees. We have washed the dishes, done the laundry, cooked and served the food, and scrubbed the floors. We even answered reservation letters on our honeymoon of three days. Duff tried to teach me how to do accounts payable, but when I paid the bills twice, he relieved me of that duty.

So what was my contribution to Stafford's success? Two things: I taught school for thirty-two years, which I loved, so that there was some income not connected to the business; and I never said "no" to any of the business adventures. Both of us were most grateful when my mother, Zona, moved in with us in 1962 to take over our household. We were so focused on making our business successful, that we did not have time to look after our children without her help. Not every business adventure was as successful as we had hoped. We did open Stafford's Patio Café in downtown Petoskey in the mid-60s. It was located on the porch outside some new shops opened behind Howard Street between the alley beneath Lake Street and Bay Street. It was Petoskey's first "outside" dining. I think we were ahead of the time for this kind of dining. There was a view of the bay, no open sky due to a canopy, and

Stafford and
Janice Smith,
2011.

often too much wind. The second year was a cold summer, and we had no way to heat the cement floor porch. So, this adventure only lasted two summers and offices now occupy the space.

After fifty years, the founder of a successful business must think of succession. Stafford's has a very loyal following with many long-term employees. Should the business be sold, passed on to the families, or could some other plan be designed whereby the corporation could continue to operate?

Stafford and Dudley had already become partners in the real estate holdings of the Pier and the Perry. So they decided to look to other key employees who contributed to the success of this operation to see if they might be interested in becoming stockholders.

Four key employees have joined Stafford and Dudley as stockholders of Stafford's Hospitality:

Christian "Butch" Paulsen started working for Stafford during high school. He became a partner in 1985 and serves as our Vice President of Purchasing.

Brian Ewbank, a second cousin of Stafford, worked at both the Pier and One Water Street. He left to manage another restaurant downstate and returned to become manager of the Weathervane in 1988. He became a partner in 2005 and is currently the Vice President of Food and Beverage, overseeing all of our restaurants.

David Marvin, Dudley's son, worked in the business during his teenage years. He became formally employed at Stafford's following his graduation from Albion College in 1997 as a manager at the Perry Hotel. He has had several positions within the company and currently serves as the Vice President and became a partner in 2005.

Gerald Gramzay, our corporate chef, joined Stafford's in 2001. With four restaurants, it became critical to hire someone to manage the quality of our food service. He became our sixth stockholder and a partner in 2011.

Stafford Reginald Smith, our eldest son, returned to the Perry Hotel as the general manager in 2008, after spending many years managing out-of-state.

These four gentlemen, and our son Reginald, will take Stafford's Hospitality into the future.

The partners of Stafford's Hospitality, Inc. Left to right: Stafford Smith, David Marvin, Brian Ewbank, Gerald Gramzay, Butch Paulsen, and Dudley Marvin.

David Marvin and Reginald Smith, second generation hoteliers.

Employee Recognition

The following employees have given at least twenty years to Stafford's Hospitality. Thank you for your many years of service!

Current Employees	Retired Staff
Stafford Smith–50 years	Louie Bandemer
Janice Smith–50 years	Ron Benson
Dudley Marvin–41 years	Pat Fowler
Darlene Marvin–41 years	Kay Griffin
Bruce Bennington–39 years	Kathleen Hart
Richard Marszalec–37 years	Dorothy Ingram
Christian (Butch) Paulsen–36 years	Janette Kalbfleisch
Ruth McCullough–36 years	Diane Kowalski
Ann Stark–36 years	Judy Mainland
Josephine (Judy) Honor–30 years	Shirley Neil
Dale Beatty–28 years	Demetra (Dee) Serva
Fred Hollerback–26 years	Steve Senglaub
Barb Diermier–25 years	Tom Ulrich
Duane Rutterbush–25 years	Lilliam Webb (deceased)
Jennifer Donker–23 years	
Phillip (Dan) Farmer–23 years	
John Still–23 years	
Mark Beer–22 years	

Special Service

Each of the Smith children, Reg, Mary-Kathryn, and Dean, have served the company intermittently over more than twenty years. Mary-Kathryn and Dean have taken different career paths and Reg remains in the company as general manager of Stafford's Perry Hotel.

Special Acknowledgment

We would like to give special acknowledgment to the current leaders of Stafford's Hospitality.

Stafford's Bay View Inn

Corey Ernst	Innkeeper
Christian (Butch) Paulsen	General Manager
Kristina Carlson	Sales and Banquet Coordinator
Richard Marszalec	Chef
Fred Hollerback	Commissary Chef

Stafford's Perry Hotel

Stafford Reginald Smith	General Manager
Winston Finlayson	Assistant General Manager
Angela Whitener	Sales Manager
Debbie Norris	Sales and Banquet Coordinator

Stafford's Pier Restaurant

Jody Ewbank	General Manager
Lindsey Walker	Assistant General Manager
Carol Parker	Dining Room Manager
Laura Vaughan	Chef

Stafford's Weathervane Restaurant

Jeff Sprecksell	General Manager
Jennifer Donker	Banquet Coordinator
Tim May	Dining Room Manager
Robert LeFurge	Chef

Corporate

Cynthia (Cindi) Bassett	Controller
Rebecca (Becky) Babcock	Marketing Coordinator
Josephine (Judy) Honor	Vice President of Hotels

Partners

Stafford Smith	Chairman
Dudley Marvin	President
David Marvin	Vice President / Chief Operating Officer
Brian Ewbank	Vice President of Food and Beverage
Christian (Butch) Paulsen	Vice President of Purchasing
Gerald Gramzay	Corporate Chef

Stafford's Hospitality Corporate Mission Statement

"To be the best hospitality business in northern Michigan;
offering exemplary service, superior quality food, beverage, and lodging
while inspiring responsible community presence."